Event Name and Date:

Guest:

E-mail or
Preferred contact:

Words:

Guest:

E-mail or
Preferred contact:

Words:

Event Name and Date:

Guest:

E-mail or
Preferred contact:

Words:

Guest:

E-mail or
Preferred contact:

Words:

Event Name and Date:

Guest:

E-mail or
Preferred contact:

Words:

Guest:

E-mail or
Preferred contact:

Words:

Event Name and Date:

Guest:

E-mail or
Preferred contact:

Words:

Guest:

E-mail or
Preferred contact:

Words:

Event Name and Date:

Guest:

E-mail or
Preferred contact:

Words:

Guest:

E-mail or
Preferred contact:

Words:

Event Name and Date:

Guest:

E-mail or
Preferred contact:

Words:

Guest:

E-mail or
Preferred contact:

Words:

Event Name and Date:

Guest:

E-mail or
Preferred contact:

Words:

Guest:

E-mail or
Preferred contact:

Words:

Event Name and Date:

Guest:

E-mail or
Preferred contact:

Words:

Guest:

E-mail or
Preferred contact:

Words:

Event Name and Date:

Guest:

E-mail or
Preferred contact:

Words:

Guest:

E-mail or
Preferred contact:

Words:

Event Name and Date:

Guest:

E-mail or
Preferred contact:

Words:

Guest:

E-mail or
Preferred contact:

Words:

Event Name and Date:

Guest:

E-mail or
Preferred contact:

Words:

Guest:

E-mail or
Preferred contact:

Words:

Event Name and Date:

Guest:

E-mail or
Preferred contact:

Words:

Guest:

E-mail or
Preferred contact:

Words:

Event Name and Date:

Guest:

E-mail or
Preferred contact:

Words:

Guest:

E-mail or
Preferred contact:

Words:

Event Name and Date:

Guest:

E-mail or
Preferred contact:

Words:

Guest:

E-mail or
Preferred contact:

Words:

Event Name and Date:

Guest:

E-mail or
Preferred contact:

Words:

Guest:

E-mail or
Preferred contact:

Words:

Event Name and Date:

Guest:

E-mail or
Preferred contact:

Words:

Guest:

E-mail or
Preferred contact:

Words:

Event Name and Date:

Guest:

E-mail or
Preferred contact:

Words:

Guest:

E-mail or
Preferred contact:

Words:

Event Name and Date:

Guest:

E-mail or
Preferred contact:

Words:

Guest:

E-mail or
Preferred contact:

Words:

Event Name and Date:

Guest:

E-mail or
Preferred contact:

Words:

Guest:

E-mail or
Preferred contact:

Words:

Event Name and Date:

Guest:

E-mail or
Preferred contact:

Words:

Guest:

E-mail or
Preferred contact:

Words:

Event Name and Date:

Guest:

E-mail or
Preferred contact:

Words:

Guest:

E-mail or
Preferred contact:

Words:

Event Name and Date:

Guest:

E-mail or
Preferred contact:

Words:

Guest:

E-mail or
Preferred contact:

Words:

Event Name and Date:

Guest:

E-mail or
Preferred contact:

Words:

Guest:

E-mail or
Preferred contact:

Words:

Event Name and Date:

Guest:

E-mail or
Preferred contact:

Words:

Guest:

E-mail or
Preferred contact:

Words:

Event Name and Date:

Guest:

E-mail or
Preferred contact:

Words:

Guest:

E-mail or
Preferred contact:

Words:

Event Name and Date:

Guest:

E-mail or
Preferred contact:

Words:

Guest:

E-mail or
Preferred contact:

Words:

Event Name and Date:

Guest:

E-mail or
Preferred contact:

Words:

Guest:

E-mail or
Preferred contact:

Words:

Event Name and Date:

Guest:

E-mail or
Preferred contact:

Words:

Guest:

E-mail or
Preferred contact:

Words:

Event Name and Date:

Guest:

E-mail or
Preferred contact:

Words:

Guest:

E-mail or
Preferred contact:

Words:

Event Name and Date:

Guest:

E-mail or
Preferred contact:

Words:

Guest:

E-mail or
Preferred contact:

Words:

Event Name and Date:

Guest:

E-mail or
Preferred contact:

Words:

Guest:

E-mail or
Preferred contact:

Words:

Event Name and Date:

Guest:

E-mail or
Preferred contact:

Words:

Guest:

E-mail or
Preferred contact:

Words:

Event Name and Date:

Guest:

E-mail or
Preferred contact:

Words:

Guest:

E-mail or
Preferred contact:

Words:

Event Name and Date:

Guest:

E-mail or
Preferred contact:

Words:

Guest:

E-mail or
Preferred contact:

Words:

Event Name and Date:

Guest:

E-mail or
Preferred contact:

Words:

Guest:

E-mail or
Preferred contact:

Words:

Event Name and Date:

Guest:

E-mail or
Preferred contact:

Words:

Guest:

E-mail or
Preferred contact:

Words:

Event Name and Date:

Guest:

E-mail or
Preferred contact:

Words:

Guest:

E-mail or
Preferred contact:

Words:

Event Name and Date:

Guest:

E-mail or
Preferred contact:

Words:

Guest:

E-mail or
Preferred contact:

Words:

Event Name and Date:

Guest:

E-mail or
Preferred contact:

Words:

Guest:

E-mail or
Preferred contact:

Words:

Event Name and Date:

Guest:

E-mail or
Preferred contact:

Words:

Guest:

E-mail or
Preferred contact:

Words:

Event Name and Date:

Guest:

E-mail or
Preferred contact:

Words:

Guest:

E-mail or
Preferred contact:

Words:

Event Name and Date:

Guest:

E-mail or
Preferred contact:

Words:

Guest:

E-mail or
Preferred contact:

Words:

Event Name and Date:

Guest:

E-mail or
Preferred contact:

Words:

Guest:

E-mail or
Preferred contact:

Words:

Event Name and Date:

Guest:

E-mail or
Preferred contact:

Words:

Guest:

E-mail or
Preferred contact:

Words:

Event Name and Date:

Guest:

E-mail or
Preferred contact:

Words:

Guest:

E-mail or
Preferred contact:

Words:

Event Name and Date:

Guest:

E-mail or
Preferred contact:

Words:

Guest:

E-mail or
Preferred contact:

Words:

Event Name and Date:

Guest:

E-mail or
Preferred contact:

Words:

Guest:

E-mail or
Preferred contact:

Words:

Event Name and Date:

Guest:

E-mail or
Preferred contact:

Words:

Guest:

E-mail or
Preferred contact:

Words:

Event Name and Date:

Guest:

E-mail or
Preferred contact:

Words:

Guest:

E-mail or
Preferred contact:

Words:

Event Name and Date:

Guest:

E-mail or
Preferred contact:

Words:

Guest:

E-mail or
Preferred contact:

Words:

Event Name and Date:

Guest:

E-mail or
Preferred contact:

Words:

Guest:

E-mail or
Preferred contact:

Words:

Event Name and Date:

Guest:

E-mail or
Preferred contact:

Words:

Guest:

E-mail or
Preferred contact:

Words:

Event Name and Date:

Guest:

E-mail or
Preferred contact:

Words:

Guest:

E-mail or
Preferred contact:

Words:

Event Name and Date:

Guest:

E-mail or
Preferred contact:

Words:

Guest:

E-mail or
Preferred contact:

Words:

Event Name and Date:

Guest:

E-mail or
Preferred contact:

Words:

Guest:

E-mail or
Preferred contact:

Words:

Event Name and Date:

Guest:

E-mail or
Preferred contact:

Words:

Guest:

E-mail or
Preferred contact:

Words:

Event Name and Date:

Guest:

E-mail or
Preferred contact:

Words:

Guest:

E-mail or
Preferred contact:

Words:

Event Name and Date:

Guest:

E-mail or
Preferred contact:

Words:

Guest:

E-mail or
Preferred contact:

Words:

Event Name and Date:

Guest:

E-mail or
Preferred contact:

Words:

Guest:

E-mail or
Preferred contact:

Words:

Event Name and Date:

Guest:

E-mail or
Preferred contact:

Words:

Guest:

E-mail or
Preferred contact:

Words:

Event Name and Date:

Guest:

E-mail or
Preferred contact:

Words:

Guest:

E-mail or
Preferred contact:

Words:

Event Name and Date:

Guest:

E-mail or
Preferred contact:

Words:

Guest:

E-mail or
Preferred contact:

Words:

Event Name and Date:

Guest:

E-mail or
Preferred contact:

Words:

Guest:

E-mail or
Preferred contact:

Words:

Event Name and Date:

Guest:

E-mail or
Preferred contact:

Words:

Guest:

E-mail or
Preferred contact:

Words:

Event Name and Date:

Guest:

E-mail or
Preferred contact:

Words:

Guest:

E-mail or
Preferred contact:

Words:

Event Name and Date:

Guest:

E-mail or
Preferred contact:

Words:

Guest:

E-mail or
Preferred contact:

Words:

Event Name and Date:

Guest:

E-mail or
Preferred contact:

Words:

Guest:

E-mail or
Preferred contact:

Words:

Event Name and Date:

Guest:

E-mail or
Preferred contact:

Words:

Guest:

E-mail or
Preferred contact:

Words:

Event Name and Date:

Guest:

E-mail or
Preferred contact:

Words:

Guest:

E-mail or
Preferred contact:

Words:

Event Name and Date:

Guest:

E-mail or
Preferred contact:

Words:

Guest:

E-mail or
Preferred contact:

Words:

Event Name and Date:

Guest:

E-mail or
Preferred contact:

Words:

Guest:

E-mail or
Preferred contact:

Words:

Event Name and Date:

Guest:

E-mail or
Preferred contact:

Words:

Guest:

E-mail or
Preferred contact:

Words:

Event Name and Date:

Guest:

E-mail or
Preferred contact:

Words:

Guest:

E-mail or
Preferred contact:

Words:

Event Name and Date:

Guest:

E-mail or
Preferred contact:

Words:

Guest:

E-mail or
Preferred contact:

Words:

Event Name and Date:

Guest:

E-mail or
Preferred contact:

Words:

Guest:

E-mail or
Preferred contact:

Words:

Event Name and Date:

Guest:

E-mail or
Preferred contact:

Words:

Guest:

E-mail or
Preferred contact:

Words:

Event Name and Date:

Guest:

E-mail or
Preferred contact:

Words:

Guest:

E-mail or
Preferred contact:

Words:

Event Name and Date:

Guest:

E-mail or
Preferred contact:

Words:

Guest:

E-mail or
Preferred contact:

Words:

Event Name and Date:

Guest:

E-mail or
Preferred contact:

Words:

Guest:

E-mail or
Preferred contact:

Words:

Event Name and Date:

Guest:

E-mail or
Preferred contact:

Words:

Guest:

E-mail or
Preferred contact:

Words:

Event Name and Date:

Guest:

E-mail or
Preferred contact:

Words:

Guest:

E-mail or
Preferred contact:

Words:

Event Name and Date:

Guest:

E-mail or
Preferred contact:

Words:

Guest:

E-mail or
Preferred contact:

Words:

Event Name and Date:

Guest:

E-mail or
Preferred contact:

Words:

Guest:

E-mail or
Preferred contact:

Words:

Event Name and Date:

Guest:

E-mail or
Preferred contact:

Words:

Guest:

E-mail or
Preferred contact:

Words:

Event Name and Date:

Guest:

E-mail or
Preferred contact:

Words:

Guest:

E-mail or
Preferred contact:

Words:

Event Name and Date:

Guest:

E-mail or
Preferred contact:

Words:

Guest:

E-mail or
Preferred contact:

Words:

Event Name and Date:

Guest:

E-mail or
Preferred contact:

Words:

Guest:

E-mail or
Preferred contact:

Words:

Event Name and Date:

Guest:

E-mail or
Preferred contact:

Words:

Guest:

E-mail or
Preferred contact:

Words:

Event Name and Date:

Guest:

E-mail or
Preferred contact:

Words:

Guest:

E-mail or
Preferred contact:

Words:

Event Name and Date:

Guest:

E-mail or
Preferred contact:

Words:

Guest:

E-mail or
Preferred contact:

Words:

Event Name and Date:

Guest:

E-mail or
Preferred contact:

Words:

Guest:

E-mail or
Preferred contact:

Words:

Event Name and Date:

Guest:

E-mail or
Preferred contact:

Words:

Guest:

E-mail or
Preferred contact:

Words:

Event Name and Date:

Guest:

E-mail or
Preferred contact:

Words:

Guest:

E-mail or
Preferred contact:

Words:

Event Name and Date:

Guest:

E-mail or
Preferred contact:

Words:

Guest:

E-mail or
Preferred contact:

Words:

Event Name and Date:

Guest:

E-mail or
Preferred contact:

Words:

Guest:

E-mail or
Preferred contact:

Words:

Event Name and Date:

Guest:

E-mail or
Preferred contact:

Words:

Guest:

E-mail or
Preferred contact:

Words:

Event Name and Date:

Guest:

E-mail or
Preferred contact:

Words:

Guest:

E-mail or
Preferred contact:

Words:

Event Name and Date:

Guest:

E-mail or
Preferred contact:

Words:

Guest:

E-mail or
Preferred contact:

Words:

Event Name and Date:

Guest:

E-mail or
Preferred contact:

Words:

Guest:

E-mail or
Preferred contact:

Words:

Event Name and Date:

Guest:

E-mail or
Preferred contact:

Words:

Guest:

E-mail or
Preferred contact:

Words:

Event Name and Date:

Guest:

E-mail or
Preferred contact:

Words:

Guest:

E-mail or
Preferred contact:

Words:

Event Name and Date:

Guest:

E-mail or
Preferred contact:

Words:

Guest:

E-mail or
Preferred contact:

Words:

Event Name and Date:

Guest:

E-mail or
Preferred contact:

Words:

Guest:

E-mail or
Preferred contact:

Words:

Event Name and Date:

Guest:

E-mail or
Preferred contact:

Words:

Guest:

E-mail or
Preferred contact:

Words:

Event Name and Date:

Guest:

E-mail or
Preferred contact:

Words:

Guest:

E-mail or
Preferred contact:

Words:

Event Name and Date:

Guest:

E-mail or
Preferred contact:

Words:

Guest:

E-mail or
Preferred contact:

Words:

Event Name and Date:

Guest:

E-mail or
Preferred contact:

Words:

Guest:

E-mail or
Preferred contact:

Words:

Event Name and Date:

Guest:

E-mail or .
Preferred contact:

Words:

Guest:

E-mail or
Preferred contact:

Words:

Event Name and Date:

Guest:

E-mail or
Preferred contact:

Words:

Guest:

E-mail or
Preferred contact:

Words:

Event Name and Date:

Guest:

E-mail or
Preferred contact:

Words:

Guest:

E-mail or
Preferred contact:

Words:

Event Name and Date:

Guest:

E-mail or
Preferred contact:

Words:

Guest:

E-mail or
Preferred contact:

Words:

Event Name and Date:

Guest:

E-mail or
Preferred contact:

Words:

Guest:

E-mail or
Preferred contact:

Words:

Event Name and Date:

Guest:

E-mail or
Preferred contact:

Words:

Guest:

E-mail or
Preferred contact:

Words:

Event Name and Date:

Guest:

E-mail or
Preferred contact:

Words:

Guest:

E-mail or
Preferred contact:

Words:

Event Name and Date:

Guest:

E-mail or
Preferred contact:

Words:

Guest:

E-mail or
Preferred contact:

Words:

Event Name and Date:

Guest:

E-mail or
Preferred contact:

Words:

Guest:

E-mail or
Preferred contact:

Words:

Event Name and Date:

Guest:

E-mail or
Preferred contact:

Words:

Guest:

E-mail or
Preferred contact:

Words:

Event Name and Date:

Guest:

E-mail or
Preferred contact:

Words:

Guest:

E-mail or
Preferred contact:

Words:

Event Name and Date:

Guest:

E-mail or
Preferred contact:

Words:

Guest:

E-mail or
Preferred contact:

Words:

Event Name and Date:

Guest:

E-mail or
Preferred contact:

Words:

Guest:

E-mail or
Preferred contact:

Words:

Made in the USA
Las Vegas, NV
01 February 2024

85184061R00070